This Is Why I Sing

SJ Sheperd

This book is dedicated to my grandfather, Robert H. Sheperd, Sr., (also fondly known as "Grpa"). He passed on his faith to me, not by many words, but just by the way he lived out his life. Thank you for teaching me, Grampa!

And, of course, to my Lord and Savior Jesus, who puts a song in my heart every day!

I also dedicate this book to Susan Scott. I would not have been able to publish this book without all of her guidance and unending patience!

Contents

SJ Sheperd's work of prose and poetry would be a rich addition to anyone's library. She knows firsthand that God is bigger than one's past and problems. A true inspirational read of praise.

~ *Suzanne G. Sheperd, BS, MA*

What a beautiful collection of Christian poetry. I found SJ's writing to be both inspirational and full of great hope. John 16:33 tells us that "In this world you will have trouble. But take heart! I have overcome the world." She shared her personal journey in this book; both the "troubles" and the joy. Each of us will have our journey in this life. But this book is a great resource to give you hope and inspiration. Thank you SJ for sharing your heart and your soul.

~ *Karen A. Gemboski, MSW*

Filled with situational memoirs, this book is sure to show how scripture is a guide.

~ *S. Ross-Legasey*
Author of "The House of Wonder"
and "The St Patrick's Day Festival."

Foreword

It has been my privilege to know SJ Sheperd for many, many years. Ours has been a journey of friendship built on similar experiences and interests, and of course, in our shared relationship with Jesus Christ, through whom we have both found much healing and comfort.

We have shared countless times of prayer, exchanged encouraging words, and inspired one another with God's workings in our personal lives. SJ has a unique relationship with Christ. She has had incredible doors open as she has just humbly sat at His feet, oftentimes not knowing what to even ask for or which direction to go. It never ceased to amaze me how God would provide answers to her, sometimes before she asked or even knew what to ask.

SJ has long had the desire to encourage and inspire others with her words. She has done this through real stories of faith, miracles, and insights, tied to scripture, to bring glory and honor to her Abba Father in heaven. It is plain to see this desire as you read through her stories and poems. Scripture says, *"Always be prepared to give an answer to everyone who asks you to give the reason for the hope that you have."* (I Peter 3:15) By picking up this book, SJ has assumed you have asked. And her answers, for the hope that she has, are found within its pages.

Written with simplicity and honesty, I hope SJ Sheperd's words will touch you as they have touched myself and many others who have had the honor of reading them. May her words bless you and remind you that you, too, can crawl into the lap of your Father in heaven and find the love and comfort you need.

With many thanks and in friendship,

Kelly Booth

Introduction

My computer died. Thank you, Jesus! (He tells us to praise Him in the good times and the bad, and this was bad.) How was I going to write a book without a computer? I thought maybe I could afford a new one but discovered that I could not.

A friend gave me a laptop to use and said I could use it as long as I needed it. She didn't like the keyboard, so she wasn't using it. The keyboard is **exactly** what I had been looking for! I can type at a good rate of speed and with minimal errors. This is just one of many stories of how the Lord can orchestrate an "8:28" (Romans 8:28 that is) which says: *"And we know that **all things work together for good** to those who love God, to those who are the called according to His purpose."* [emphasis added].

Even though there may be a trial, God can make something good come out of it. I have seen it over and over again. That is why I have devoted an entire chapter titled: **God Can "8:28" It!** Once you read these stories, it is my hope that you will learn to keep your eyes and ears open to the 8:28's He does in your life. The Holy Spirit is continually at work within and around us. Sometimes the Holy Spirit speaks in a soft whisper or in events that happen in our lives. My poem, "Voice of the Shepherd" illustrates how we need to STOP, LOOK and LISTEN for His presence. And once we get closer, we can actually hear the Holy Spirit speaking to us.

You will also read about examples of what a God-cidence is. There is no such thing as a coincidence. Things we call a coincidence are actually God's way of speaking into our lives and I call them a God-cidence. You will find a chapter based on the way I have seen God working in my life in this way.

"Miracles are never meant to be ends in and of themselves. Miracles are meant to point beyond themselves to the Miracle Worker. What makes a real difference is how well we know the One to whom these miracles point. That makes all the difference in the world."[1]

_____

[1] *Taken from "The 52 Greatest Stories of the Bible," by*

As you will see, I have been blessed in so many ways, and that is why I sing. It is my prayer that as you read this book, it will spur you on to realizing that you, too, have reasons to sing! Another exciting thing we can learn is in *Zephaniah 3:17. It* says, *"The Lord your God in your midst, the Mighty One, will save, He will rejoice over you with gladness, He will quiet you with His love, He will rejoice over you with singing,"* Not only do we sing out to the Lord, but He is also doing the same thing for us!

•

"Sing to Him, sing psalms to Him. Talk of all His wondrous works! – Psalm 105:2

Kenneth Boa and John Alan Turner Kenneth Boa and John Alan Turner

Waiting to Be Found

I wrote the following poem in 1993. My children were very young at the time (3 yrs., 2 yrs., and an infant). Suffice it to say, I was a little busy. I thoroughly enjoyed my career as a stay-at-home mother. I have many fond memories: marching around the house in a parade to the sound of patriotic music, creating with Play Dough or splashing in the puddles after a rainstorm (in our bathing suits).

During this time, I had a Spiritual Adviser. I explained to her that I was so exhausted that I fell asleep anytime I began to pray. She put me at ease when she said that God knows I'm busy and He understands. It was at this point she gave me a precious and life-transforming piece of advice. "Just go about your day and pray as you go. Pray while you are doing the dishes, while doing your laundry..."

Because of that advice, I have learned to be in constant communion with Him, even now, as I go throughout my day. Back then, I began getting up before my family awoke for the day, in order to spend time in God's Word. Out of that time, I began writing this poem, as I thirsted to hear from God more intimately.

~ "Ask and it will be given to you; seek and you will find; knock, and it will be opened to you. For everyone who asks receives, and he who seeks finds, and to him who knocks it will be opened."

~ Matthew 7:7

Voice of the Shepherd

Shhh! Do you hear Me? ...Close your eyes,
and you will hear Me.

Shhh! Do you see Me? ...Look inside,
and you will see Me.

Shhh! Do you feel Me? ...Be still,
and you will feel Me.

I'm in your heart – just waiting to be found.

Turn off the TV – Turn off the radio – Turn off the useless talk.

I need to be heard – you need to hear Me.

<u>Then</u> you will find love. <u>Then</u> you will find peace.

<u>Then</u> you will find true happiness and joy.

Fear not... for you have been called by name.

Listen to the story – made just for you.

Shhh! Stop and hear your story.

Shhh! Be still and feel your story.

Arise! Then <u>live</u> your story!

Fear not, for I am with you always...

Listen to the voice of the Shepherd.

Words Have Power

"The Lord merely spoke, and the heavens were created. He breathed the Word and all the stars were born." ~ Psalm 33:6 (NLT)

The Words of the Bible have the most power of all. The words are alive and relevant, bringing healing, and other powerful changes in the life of the reader.

In the very first verse of Genesis, it says that God <u>spoke</u> the world into existence. it begins with these powerful words: *"In the beginning*

God created the heavens and the earth..." How did He create? He simply <u>spoke</u> things into existence. In verses 3-5, it says: *"Then God said, "Let there be light," and there was light. And God saw the light, that it was good, and God divided the light from the darkness. God called the light Day and the darkness He called Night. So, the evening and the morning were the first day."* He did the same thing while creating the rest of the universe. He spoke the water into existence, along with land, trees, animals, and so on.

Further along, in chapter 1, verses 26-28, God continues with His awesome creating. It says: *"Let Us make man in Our image, according to Our likeness...So God created man in His own image, in the image of God He created him, male and female He created them. Then God blessed them..."*

Did you pick up on who He created man to be like? It says, *"Let **Us** make man in **Our** image..."* 'Us and Our' refer to the Father, the Son, and the Holy Spirit. Amazing, isn't it?

Words can create life-altering results. It has been said that a minimum of 5 positive words of affirmation are needed to get rid of the effects of 1 negative comment. This is proof that we need to encourage one another and be mindful of what we say to each other.

Chalkboard Dream

I was standing on the lip of a huge chalkboard, walking across from the left to the right, holding onto the wall for dear life. As I did, there were words of discouragement all over it; words like... loser... you're ugly... you're no good.

Once I got to the end, I began to walk from the right to the left. This time was different though. There were words again, but they had changed to positive and encouraging words like... you're beautiful.... you're kind... you're worthy...

Unlike the negative words I was being called, I felt like Jesus was telling me who I really was in His sight, and that He loves me just as I am.

Sticks & Stones

Psalm 91:21 (NLT) says, "This I declare of the Lord: He alone is my refuge, my place of safety; He is my God, and I am trusting Him."

They say names don't hurt,
but what do they know?
They cause so much pain,
and resentments to grow.

Self-esteem is a problem,
but we can get it back.
With Christ at our center,
He'll put us on track.

God pays attention
to all of us here.
He adores and upholds us,
to Him we are dear.

Speak kindly to all.
Uplift one another.
'Cause after all,
we're 'sister and brother.'

Life on this earth's short —
it's gone in an instant,
Don't stay for the abuse,
it's all right to be distant.

There are times when it's best
for you not to stay.
When he tells you 'Come home,'
just say, "There's no way!"

I pray my dream and this poem will bring hope to you if you find yourself in a similar situation. You are not alone. Others, like myself, have gone before you, and you will find your way too. Not only that, but Jesus is right there in your midst.

One Word

I had just finished reading an article written by Debbie Macomber. In it she said, "Each year I choose one word to focus on and live by." After reading about this practice, I prayed, "God, I wish I could have a wor..." 'perseverance'... just like that, a still small voice answered before I could even finish my prayer. That year, everywhere I turned, the word perseverance was found. It usually came at times when I really needed to be encouraged to persevere.

Since then, some other words that I have chosen are: Prosper, Hope, Obey, Restore and Thrive. Obey may seem like a negative word, but it wasn't. Very often, the word trust came along with it: Trust & Obey. The Lord was teaching me how to live a surrendered life for Him. Miraculously, during the year of the word Restore, not one, but two relationships in my life were restored. God is amazing!

"The Word of God is living and powerful..."
~ Hebrews 4:12

Healed

I am on many medications because of an illness. On more than one occasion, I thought I was 'healed' and proceeded to stop taking my medications. Each time, it was not the right thing to do, my health deteriorated, and I would end up in the hospital.

One day, when a friend and I were talking. I told him how I wished I could be healed of this illness. His response to me was, "You _are healed_, as long as you _stay_ on your medications!" Because of his words, I have not gone off my medications since that day. His words were literally lifesaving.

Some of My Thoughts

"If you're open and seeking, God will lead."

"In order to believe, there needs to be a dream."

"He did it once – He can do it again!" (Like the parting of the Red Sea and the Jordan River)

"We need to walk, looking to pick up God's 'scent,' in order to follow His lead; like a dog does, searching for his Master."

"A snowflake is harmless by itself, but more than one can accumulate into something really

11

big. ~ It's the same way with cookies – one here and another one there seem harmless but can accumulate into something really big too."

"I have greater plans for you, don't doubt it one minute. From your trials will come joy if you just keep Me in it." (Taken from my poem 'Significant')

"We're all on a path that we take with our feet. Yet our spirit will yearn, 'til it's You that we meet." (Taken from my poem 'Time for Truth')

"You are my Savior, my one and only. It's You who's there when I'm down and lonely." (Taken from my poem 'You')

"Write to Jesus and be Right with Jesus."

"There is JOY in the JOurneY"

'God-fidence' (A term I came up with because my confidence comes from God.)

What's a God-cidence?

There is no such thing as a coincidence. It's a God-cidence. What does that mean? It is God's way of making things out of the ordinary happen; things that only He could design. They are all around us, we just need to become more aware of them. They are little reminders that God is involved in every detail of our lives, whether big, or small. I have listed a few examples to help you get a better understanding of what I mean.

In His Hands

Both my sons were in the Navy and one of them was stationed in Japan. One day he called to tell me that he had just moved, to be stationed in Guam. Two weeks later the tsunami happened in Japan. Its effects were also felt in Guam but were minor. The sailors had moved up to the top of the island where they were safely kept.

Coincidence? No... it's a God-cidence!

My daughter, along with my son, had shared an apartment together in Georgia. Then at one point, they both moved away. My son was stationed in New York state and my daughter moved to Massachusetts. They both moved, shortly before Hurricane Matthew struck that area. God was, once again, protecting my children.

Coincidence? No... it's a God-cidence!

Empty Jar

I was in the process of going through a divorce. I had moved into my grandfather's house until I could get out on my own. Things were tough though; I didn't have a job and my money was running out. It got so bad that one day I had to empty out my jar of coins in order to pay for my prescriptions... but it wasn't enough. I broke down and called the church I attended and told them about my situation. They said they could help me. As a policy, they don't just hand money out, which I can totally understand. So, one of the Deacons at the church picked me up and we went to the pharmacy where he paid for my prescriptions.

I was still having a difficult time and was not able to relax. A friend suggested that I put on a Christian radio station, as I slept. Then when I woke up during the night, I was blessed by hearing the lyrics to a song, which said, *"God will take care of you... through everyday... o'er all the way. He will care for you... God will take care of you."* I peacefully went back to sleep.

Coincidence? No... it's a God-cidence!

In the Margin

I had a dream where I was going up a hill in a neighborhood. As I did, there were people cheering, as they hung out their windows and some were also out in their front yards. Then, I began to be pulled back and was upset because I wanted to go see my grandfather, who was in heaven.

I guess it wasn't time for me to go to heaven yet, but it gave me peace knowing that one day I will. I was considering whether I was going to put this dream in the book. Then, later, I went to my Bible and there was a pen inside the pages. In the margin of the page, I had written about that same exact dream.

Coincidence? No... it's a God-cidence!

Tell Everyone

One day, as I was writing this book, I was hearing things like, "What are you doing? You're wasting your time. You're never going to finish it. You won't get it published." I proceeded to ignore those thoughts and kept on writing. Then, later on in the day, a friend called me. She asked me if she could read Psalm 99 to me. I asked her if she could hold on, so I could get my Bible to follow along with her.

When I opened up to that page, there was one sentence that I had highlighted previously. It said: *"Publish His glorious deeds among the nations. Tell everyone about the amazing things He does." ~ Psalm 96:3 (NLT)*

Coincidence? No... it's a God-cidence!

Jesus Sends an Angel

I had been in the hospital for 49 days. Because of that, I was unable to pay my rent and I lost my apartment. I was definitely at a very low point in my life. The hospital could not release me until they found a place to send me.

That place ended up being a homeless shelter, in the middle of a city where I did not feel very safe. After such an extended amount of time in the hospital, I was really nervous. I was really withdrawn, and afraid to trust anyone.

We were able to sleep overnight at the shelter, but after breakfast we had to leave for the day and not return again, until suppertime.

I was blessed that I still had my car, so I was able to go places during the day, like the library or malls, for example.

At the shelter there were volunteers who also worked the evening shift. The second night I recognized one of the women. She was a favorite teacher of mine when I was in 5th grade! She sat with me on the couch, and I poured out my heart to her as I told her my story on how I ended up there. She just sat with her arm around me and listened. She 'loved on me,' and I was able to begin my healing process. The teacher proved that <u>no words</u> could have power too!

Coincidence? No... it's a God-cidence!

Where Are They?

Two pages of my yearly devotional book had been torn out. I was on my second year of reading it. I had found one page and put it into its rightful place. But the time was coming when

I would need the page for September 20th and 21st. I had absolutely no idea where it was. I had known for about 2 months that I would need those days. Then, on September 19th, the day before I needed it, I opened a notebook, and the pages were right there tucked inside a pocket in the folder. Now don't try to tell me that God isn't interested in even the smallest details of our lives.

Coincidence? No... it's a God-cidence!

"Me!"

I helped a lot taking care of my cousin's daughter. She was learning how to talk and called me "Me". We could not figure out why. Until one day we realized what was happening. When her mother was playing with her, she would say, "Do you want to help <u>Mommy</u> put this puzzle together?" Then her father would say, "Can you show <u>Daddy</u> your new doll?"

When I was with her, I would say, "Can you give <u>me</u> a hug?" I referred to myself as 'me', instead of by my name. So, she thought Me was my name.

One day, when she was about 3 years old, we were playing, and she went into her bedroom and closed the door. Little did I know, there was a lock on the doorknob. I didn't know what I was going to do. She started calling, "Me! Me!"

I knew what I **didn't** want to do, and that was call her mother. As I prayed, the doorbell rang. I went downstairs and it was a woman with a package. I asked her if she could help me. She followed me upstairs and in a matter of seconds, opened the door by using a credit card! I couldn't thank her enough.

See? God is always there to help. Sometimes He even delivers a package right on time!

Coincidence? No... it's a God-cidence!

As the Deer...

While visiting my friend, she took me down her hallway to show me a special painting on her wall. It had a brook and three deer on it. Two of the deer were on the left side of the brook, while one deer was on the right side. She told me that she really liked deer and commented on the lone deer. She said what it meant to her was she was the deer on the right side of the brook, waiting to cross to the other side. She said it wasn't time yet for her to go to the other side yet (heaven). The painting was of a winter scene that said, *As the deer pants for streams of water, so my soul pants for you, O God.*

After our visit, I got into my car. On the radio was a song with the following lyrics: *"As the deer panteth for the water, so my soul longeth after thee..."*

Coincidence? No... it's a God-cidence!

I Lift My Voice

I was in the hospital, and it was pretty serious this time. I was unresponsive so they had to do all sorts of tests on me to discover what my problem was. While in this state, I heard my cousin singing a song in my right ear. I also felt the presence of my aunt on my left. After coming out of it, I asked my cousin what song she was singing to me. She said she could not believe that I heard her. Our friend had told her to keep talking to me, that I could hear her.

She told me what the song was. Here are the lyrics:

"I love You Lord, and I lift my voice,
To worship You, O my soul, rejoice.
Take joy my King, in what You hear,
Let it be a sweet, sweet sound in your ear."

It was a sweet, sweet sound in **my** ear!

Sometime later...I was talking with a friend of mine. He was telling me a story about when he was in a Bible Study. They were in a circle holding hands as they sang, and he said it brought tears to his eyes. It was very moving for him. The song? *"I Love You Lord, and I Lift My Voice..."*

Coincidence? No... it's a God-cidence!

Who Was Here?

My son was living in Georgia. One day he was getting into his car, when a gentleman stopped him. He wanted to know where he had gotten the design on his car. You see, my daughter learned at her trade high school, how to design and put stickers on things. My son had a dent in the side of his Mustang and my daughter made a clever use for it. She put a sticker over the dent that was a picture of a boot print mark (like someone had kicked the dent into the car). Above it, she put the words: Chuck Norris was here!

The gentleman said he needed someone with that talent in his shop and said he would like to meet her. Sounds simple – but it wasn't. She was living in Massachusetts. Before I knew it, I was driving her to the airport so she could go to Georgia for an interview, and soon thereafter, she moved out of state into a new adventure!

Coincidence? No... it's a God-cidence!

He's There in The Laundry

I was doing laundry and had been reading a book while waiting. It was all about Matthew 6:33-34. The book was talking about worry and how we lose faith when we worry. We are not trusting in God. When I was waiting for some clothes to dry, I decided to go through my emails. I have a site that sends me a 'verse of the day.' Of course, the Lord was speaking to me through it. It was in *Matthew 6:34,* which says, *"Therefore do not worry about tomorrow, for tomorrow will worry about its own things. Sufficient for the day is its own trouble."* I guess He doesn't want me to worry!

Coincidence? No... it's a God-cidence!

God Can "8:28" It

Romans 8:28 that is – which says:
And we know that ___all things work together for good___ ___to those who love God,___ *to those who are the called according to His purpose.* [emphasis added].

Even though there may be a trial, God can make something good come out of it. I have seen it over and over again. That is why I am devoting an entire chapter to **God Can "8:28" It!** Once you read these stories, it is my hope that you will learn to keep your eyes and ears open to the 8:28's He does in your life.

Chairs Not Included

I needed to find an apartment as soon as possible. I was not going to be able to pay next month's rent, where I was living. I immediately went to Craig's List to find an apartment I could afford.

Little did I know, the Lord was going to 8:28 this. I found an apartment that was ready for me to move in at any time. There was one problem though, all I had for furniture was a love seat and a kitchen table (chairs not included).

Again, God did an 8:28. There was a woman at church who needed to get rid of some furniture. Her grandmother passed away and she now had a house full of furniture – literally. We could barely walk around inside the house. She was so anxious to get rid of it, that she gave all of it to me for free!

I left there with a twin bed (perfect for me — I'm single and it takes up less space), a bureau, a living room chair that rocked and swiveled, a TV stand (I don't have a TV)[2] and a desk big

---

[2] *As I explained, I did not have a TV to put on the stand. That was okay though, I didn't watch it very often. Then one day, a close friend told me that when her daughter heard that I didn't*

enough for a computer and a printer.

All I needed to do was buy some kitchen chairs and one for the desk as well.

On Holy Ground

I had been in the hospital for over a month. During that time, I was scared and lonely. All my friends and family were an hour away from the hospital. I didn't trust anyone there. Eventually, I discovered that I could request to have the pastor visit me.

I met with him and was put at ease right away. He was someone I could relax with; someone I could trust… We had many visits together. One time he brought me lyrics to some songs, so I could sing, be comforted, and feel God's presence while I was alone. That was such a blessing.

Also, during that time, I had a very vivid dream:

I was walking barefoot on a straight path set before

---

have a TV, she said: "That's just not right Mom!" Before I knew it, a flat screen TV was delivered to my doorstep. I didn't even ask, yet still I received!

me. It was lined with a carpet of soft, brown pine needles. On either side of the path there was a single row of pinecones lining it. I didn't see them, but I could feel the protective covering of trees over me. I was on holy ground and at total peace. I saw a brook in the distance. It, too, was straight and narrow. Other than the brook, everything was bright white. As I got closer, I noticed a woman crouched down on the other side, with her hand extended out to me. She was encouraging me to come closer. As I did, I noticed that the woman's skirt was flowing with swirls of all different colors – mostly shades of blue, pink, gray and white.

As I was telling all this to the pastor, he asked me who I thought the woman was. "My guardian angel," I replied. The pastor just smiled. Then he asked me if the water was deep. "No, she told me it wasn't," I said. I didn't hear a voice though, it was a 'knowing,' a conveying of thoughts, and that was the only thing she told me.

Then, just as I was about to step onto one of the rocks in the brook... I woke up. I guess it wasn't time for me to cross to the other side yet. I must have work here to do first. But I was comforted knowing what was on the other side when my time does come. To me, the dream also gave me assurance that I would be fine with my next move. You see, I needed to find an Assisted Living place, and was scared about the whole situation.

Out of the horrible experience in the hospital, I gained a new friend. He helped me just by taking the time to listen. That's exactly what I needed. As I spoke to him, I was able to solve some questions on my own. He hardly had to tell me anything, his listening ear was great medicine. Pills are not the only thing that can cure! God did another 8:28

How About Today?

I needed to find another apartment, again! I wouldn't be able to afford where I was living. I could only pay rent for two more months. I had no idea what I was going to do – but God knew! He was going to 8:28 this. He taught me to put my total trust in Him.

Five years prior, I had put my name on many wait lists for housing in many surrounding towns (about 5 or 6 of them). During those years, I prayed to God about wanting to live in one particular town.

One day I received a call from one of the

places where I had applied. They asked if I would be willing to look at an apartment that was available. When I asked if next week would be okay, their response was "How about **today**?" Well, I decided that was a good idea and went there that same day.

I really liked it. It was very bright inside, which is especially important to me. If it is too dark, it brings my mood down. So, before I knew it, I was signing papers to move into a new apartment! I was blessed with a month-to-month lease, where I was currently living so I was able to give them notice that I was going to be moving without having to break a lease. Everything happened so fast. I was packed and moved in within two weeks.

During my many moves, God has provided me with people to help me move, who would not accept any money or food or even a drink. Jesus is my awesome Provider! I know He is preparing a Home for me in Heaven. But He also keeps preparing me homes here on earth. I can gratefully say that I have not had to move since 2013, which, as of this writing, has been 8 years.

Psalm 37:4 says, *"Delight thyself also in the*

Lord, and He shall give thee the desires of thine heart." (That verse has been engraved on my checkbook cover for many, many years. And He has done that many, many times as well.)

So, God, once again, gave me an 8:28 - I did not know where I was going to be able to move to on such short notice. God, in essence, said: Here you go – oh, and by the way, I am going to give you "the desire of your heart" – an apartment in the town that you have prayed for.

No Show

I was hosting an event and we were to meet at a local restaurant before going out to another activity. I arrived at the restaurant early and bought a newspaper. Inside was an article regarding a Toastmasters group. They were offering 4 classes for a total of $6.00 at a local library. Well, this is where God did an 8:28. No one showed up for the event. But I never would have found out about the Toastmasters if I hadn't gone to the restaurant. I ended up attending the meetings and they were very enriching.

In Good Times and In Bad

I was in a car accident where I was hit from behind. I immediately yelled out "Thank You, Jesus!" (We are taught to praise Him in the good times, and in the bad - so I did). Two friends came to pick me up, since I was a little shaken up. From that accident, my car was totaled. With the money that the insurance company gave me, God did an 8:28. I was then able to buy another car for cash!

Laundry Room Surprise

I went to the laundry room where I live, to clean some clothes and sheets. When I got there, all of the machines were being used, so I had to leave. Then I remembered the other laundry room at another building that I could go to.

When I arrived, all the machines were available. That wasn't the best part though – there was a small CD player on the counter with a FREE sign on it! So, I took it home. There was no cord so it would need to be run on batteries. That was fine by me. I opened up where the batteries were located to see what I would need.

It was full of batteries, but there was one problem – 2 of the batteries had exploded. That wasn't going to stop me though. I took them out and cleaned inside the player. I then went to where I keep my batteries in the closet. I had doubts that I had any C-size batteries, never mind have 6 of them. I was surprised at finding 8 of them! Once I put in the new batteries, and pushed the start button, it worked!! Another 8:28!

Praise the Lord, call upon His name; declare His deeds among the peoples make mention that His name is exalted. Sing to the Lord, for He has done excellent things; this is known in all the earth. Cry out and shout, O inhabitant of Zion, for great is the Holy One of Israel in your midst!"

~ Isaiah 12:4-6

Miracles

The countdown to a miracle began on another typical cool and crisp, winter evening in New England. I was enjoying my time with a few friends in a warm and cozy home. I then came up with what I thought was a great idea. A new skating rink was opening up behind the City Hall and I wanted to go. Only one other person agreed to go along with me. Once there, we had to wait in line for 45 minutes to rent our pair of skates.

After getting the skates, I sat down to put

them on. They were unlike any I had ever seen before. Instead of having laces to tighten them around my ankles, they buckled. They were like ski boots on blades. They were not snug at all. I struggled to walk over to the rink. My feet were wobbling around inside, but I just kept going on ahead.

Once I was on the ice, I immediately headed for the wall of the rink to have something to hold onto. I almost made it but fell down on the way. Once I recovered myself, I was successful at reaching my destination and felt more secure.

I was perfectly happy right where I was, but my friend decided to pull me away from the safety of the wall, into the center of the rink, saying, "That's not how you skate, you need to come out here!" After he did that, he proceeded to take off skating. Soon thereafter, I did what I knew best – I fell. This time was different though. I found out that ice is hard and unforgiving!

A couple came over to see if I was ok, I wasn't. I had this strange feeling about my hand. I looked and saw that it was hanging down at the wrist. Definitely broken! So much for a night of skating. I didn't even make it halfway across the rink! My friend returned our skates and then off we went to the hospital.

Upon arriving at the emergency room, a woman was there to check me in. She had a look of fear on her face as she picked up the phone to the staff in the emergency room. She asked if they could take me in - 'like now?' I guess the sight of my hand dangling really had her concerned. I was rushed into a room so quickly that she did not even have time to ask me my name.

Not long after, a doctor and nurse came over and had a look at my wrist. The doctor was speaking to me about my situation. He was using all kinds of fancy words that made no sense. I then proceeded to ask him, "Do you mean that you are going to have to re-set it?" He said yes, and that it was going to hurt... a lot! "What if I scream?" I asked. He said, "You wouldn't be the first one." ~ Oh, great!

At that point I noticed that someone was closing the glass partition doors - I suppose so no one would be able to hear me. So, then I said, "Ahh, do you think we could pray about this before you do it?" He said, "Yes, do you want to hold my hand?" I did and then I proceeded to pray and asked God to give the doctor wisdom for what he needed to do.

After praying, the nurse said to me, "Hold onto my hand and squeeze it as tight as you need to. That is what I'm here for."

Then the doctor said, "OK, I'm going to give you a countdown, so you will be prepared and know when I am going to do it."

"Ok, 3 – 2 – 1 …." I immediately used the breathing method I learned while giving birth to my 3 children: Breathe in slowly through the nose – then exhale slowly out through the mouth... in through the nose and out through the mouth...in through…

"OK, I'm done!" he said. "You are?!" I replied astonishingly!

The doctor then said, "Yes, and I've done a lot of these and I have <u>never</u> seen anyone react the way you just did!" I smiled and cheered as I said, "That's God!" There was absolutely no pain! I could tell when he aligned the bones up, but I didn't feel anything. I'm not sure how to describe it. I had no reason to scream like we had all anticipated I would!

Now, not only was I going to tell everyone this story, I knew that the doctor, the nurse and the woman who checked me in, would probably do the same... spreading the news that Jesus is still in the healing business.

Well, the 'easy' part was done. Now I needed to wait for the swelling to go down before anything would be done. That was the first step. Eventually, a doctor performed the surgery. A metal plate was put inside since I had shattered the bones. God was good though, my left hand was broken, not my right hand, which is the one I use the most. Now I had work ahead of me to do.

A good friend let me stay at her place while I was beginning to heal. She helped me to get dressed, and every other thing that I was unable to do for myself now. Somehow, we were able to get me dressed up to go to a Christian Singles Christmas Party. Fortunately, the dress and jacket fit over my hand, and I was able to go out.

Then the Lord provided me with an awesome gift. I was eligible for assistance from a home health aide! The woman came 3 days a week. She helped me with my bathing, dressing, dishes, and so on.

As far as recovery went, I had to go to physical therapy shortly after the surgery.

Because of my hand being immobile for such a long time, my fingers were not able to bend correctly anymore. Therefore, I had exercises that I needed to do to bring them back to their original function.

I was faithful at going to physical therapy and doing the exercises I was told to do. At one point though, I have to admit, I was really down and feeling hopeless. Would the pain ever go away? Would I ever be able to get the full use of my hand back again? One night, I was over a friend's house, and I had fallen asleep on the couch. I woke up crying because of the pain and the disappointing feeling I had about things ever getting back to normal. My friend came over to me to soothe me. She reminded me of how I was moving forward with my progress and needed to focus on that – not on how far I had to go. She was right. That was a turning point for me.

One of the exercises that I did, was to hold my hand in a fist position, with the thumb holding all the other fingers down. Then I was to move the thumb and keep the fist in place. I was able to do that with all of my fingers, except one. Every time I did the exercise, my pointer finger would immediately spring up. I was beginning to get discouraged, but I continued with my therapy, as I had been instructed.

After weeks of beginning the therapy, another miracle happened. This time, when I made the fist, my pointer finger didn't move when I took the thumb away! I was so excited that I called my physical therapist to tell her the good news! She was as excited as I was. From that point on, my recovery continued, and I moved forward with my healing progress.

Years later, I am happy to say that I have fully recovered. My left hand performs as well as my right hand. I am even able to open jars without a problem. Out of this experience, I have learned that I never would have been able to cope with this injury if I didn't have the Lord to lean on. I also learned that if I could persevere (there's that word again) and work alongside God, I could get fantastic results.

I have to admit, I am much more careful of my 'great ideas'. I go for the safer activities now. I'm not as agile as I used to be. But I am still a kid at heart. Now I try to do safer things like miniature golfing and going for walks. I am not a runner though. I would probably fall if I tried to – and we all know how graceful I am when

I fall.

*"You thrill me Lord, with all You have done for me.
I sing for joy because of what you have done."*
~ Psalm 92:4 (NLT)

Leaving the Church

I was a teacher at our church. The children from my class, including my son, were receiving their first communion. There were two masses that they were going to be in. My son was going to be in the second one; but I wanted to see my other students at the first mass, because I had a small gift for each of them. After the children went inside, I left, since I would be returning.

As I was walking to my car, in the rain, I had my umbrella open. All of a sudden, lightning struck! There were two other women in the parking lot at that time. All of our umbrellas went flying up into the air, as the lightning traveled up our arms and into the handle of the umbrellas!

One woman started laughing hysterically and the other woman began crying hysterically. My response was to run up the hill and give the crying woman a hug to soothe her.

At the same time, car alarms began to go off, the traffic signals started blinking and the school's power was affected, along with their telephones.

I thought you were supposed to get hit by lightning when you <u>entered</u> a church; I was <u>leaving</u>! The two women pulled me back into the church. We went to a pew but did not pay any attention to the service. We were so giddy and 'electrified'.

It was a summer with many storms. When it was lightning out, I stayed inside because of my new-found fear. But eventually I told myself that I needed to face my fear and returned outside during a storm. This time without an umbrella though!

It's My Angel

It was Christmastime and I was with a couple of friends at a restaurant. We were celebrating and sharing some gifts. Mine, though, was far beyond the best. It was an angel – she looked just like the guardian angel in my dream!

The angel was a little over a foot tall, and beautiful. She had a skirt made of glass, and inside the skirt it was filled with water and little sparkles. When I turned it on, all the sparkles began to float around and change colors. There were times that the colors matched the skirt of the angel in my dream! God is such a wonderful gift-giver!

Protected

"Come and see what our God has done, what awesome miracles He does for His people."
~ Psalm 66:5 (NLT)

- One day I was lighting a candle. I had on a pink and white fluffy sweater. As I struck the match, my sweater caught on fire. The flames started at the bottom of the sweater and went straight up toward my face, but immediately went out. There was absolutely no sign of the sweater being burnt and I was not harmed. My God protected me!

- We lived in a 3-decker apartment when I survived a quick call. As I pulled the chain on the back hallway light bulb, it exploded and glass went everywhere, but I was not hurt at all. I should have gotten glass in my eyes, as I was looking up! My God protected me again!

- We went to the local fairgrounds, and they offered rides in a Cessna airplane. While in the air, we discovered that the door next to my son was not closed tightly. God protected him until we were able to land. Thank You, Jesus!

- One of my sons had worked all day, into the early hours of the following morning. At 5 AM he was on his way home, but almost didn't make it. He fell asleep at the wheel while on the highway. While going 55mph, he collided with another car in the left-hand lane. Miraculously, no one was injured! God was protecting my family again and this was a really big one! Thank You, Jesus!

"I will praise You, O Lord, with my whole heart, I will tell of all Your marvelous works. I will be glad and rejoice in You. I will sing praises to Your name, O Most High." ~ Psalm 9:1-2

Rhyme Time

One hot, humid, summer day, my friend and I were sitting on her front porch, just trying to stay cool, but not having any success. That is, until Jesus sent us a _downpour_ of rain. We were so hot, that we didn't care that we were getting soaked. As a matter of fact, we ran into the front yard to cool off. That experience was the inspiration for this poem.

Joy in the Rain

Turning & turning with my hands held high.
If they don't know You, then they wonder why.

Joyful & giddy at being your daughter,
it's so much fun to play in Your water.

On the days when I see a rainbow is here,
I'm reminded of the promise that You
made so clear.

Some think we worship only down our knees.
I like dancing and singing, and I think
You are pleased.

Can't wait 'till the day when I see
with my eyes,
I don't know the details; it'll be a surprise.

When Your roll call comes, it will be a fine day.
'cause the truth is true:
it's You who does Reign!

*"...and they lived and reigned with Christ for a
thousand years" ~ Rev. 20:4*

I wrote this next poem when my mind was racing and would not slow down. So, I asked God to help me cope.

Turn on the Quiet

Quiet my mind, Lord, amidst this hurried race,
Bring me peace and serenity,
as I adjust to Your pace.

Time is of the essence, but not as the world sees.
Relationships with others,
is the way You aim to please.

Every person that we come across, was put here
just by You, and you always have a purpose for
putting them in view.

Sometimes it's for them, sometimes it's for us.
But find out the truth, is something we must.

We're all on a path that we take with our feet.
Yet our spirit will yearn, 'til it's
You that we meet!

"Oh come, let us worship and bow down; let us kneel before the Lord our Maker. For He is our God, and we are the people of His pasture, and the sheep of His hand."
~ Psalm 95:6-7

Today or Tomorrow

Time with Christ is what I crave,
it's all from Him when I am brave.

Be it today or be it tomorrow,
soon there won't be any more sorrow.

Thankful for how He makes my way,
I'm eagerly waiting for that perfect day.

Today is a day I am so grateful for,
whether there's a few, or many more.

Writing poems, He works through me,
He gives me words to make me see.

No matter the creed or even the race.
We're all given the chance to seek out His face.

One fine day the trumpet will sound,
at Home with Him is where I'll be found.

Spending time everlasting is what I long for.
Accept Jesus Christ when He knocks on your door.

*"And God will wipe away every tear from their eyes, there
shall be no more death, nor sorrow, nor crying. There shall be
no more pain, for the former things have passed away."*
~ Revelation 21:4

The following poem was written after a scary experience. I was being trained for a job driving a van. We were to bring some people to a day program for the elderly at a local church.

We had already dropped everyone off and were on our way back to the office when we were at a stop light. All of a sudden, a fire engine pulled out of its station with sirens blaring. It came on our side of the street and almost hit us! The driver told me afterwards, that although we had been in the left lane, he heard a voice, telling him to move over to the right lane. If he had not moved, we would have been hit head on! Once we got to our destination, we took the time to pray and thank God for His protection over us.

When I got home, I picked up a pen and paper. And, as fast as that fire engine was heading toward us, is how fast the poem came out of me. I wrote it in about 10 minutes! It was definitely the Holy Spirit working through me.

Transitions

Transitions come. Transitions go.
Sometimes fast. Sometimes slow.

Some change our lives forever,
(for better or for worse)
And we don't always know if
they're a blessing or a curse.

They can happen in an instant,
or slowly over time.
But one thing I am certain of,
God's team is on our side.

If we just love and work with
the people that we meet,
It's God's way of helping to turn the
bitter into sweet.

*"For He shall give His angels charge over you, to
keep you in all your ways" ~ Psalm 91:11*

You

It's You who is the Author of my lifelong story,
as I listen and live, to You goes the glory.

You are my Savior, my one and only,
it's You who's there when I'm down and lonely.

Praise, honor, and love is what You are due.
You make me feel I'm number one to You.

Each day is different, it's never the same.
Hallelujah for that; You know me by name.

We've been through so much, and
time has just flown.
You said I would prosper and it's how
I have grown.

Don't want to be bitter because of the pain.
You're there in the sun and there in the rain.

You guide and direct me every step of the way.
Staying true to You. I try to each day.

Philippians, Ephesians, You wrote through Paul.
The Psalms, Isaiah, I love them all.

It's not really me, it's You who's the author.
I'm so glad I can say that I am your daughter.

Changed

We're calling for You Lord,
in the middle of the night.
Life has changed for everyone,
it's time to do what's right.

We're lost and we don't know
exactly what to do,
Desperate for some answers
we're crying out to you,

You love the ones who love you,
You love the ones who don't.
Each one has a chance to choose You,
some will - but some just won't.

Time is of the essence,
it's beginning to unwind.
We don't want to be lost here,
it's You we need to find.

A kind and loving Father
is who You really are.
Are you near to us, dear Lord?
Or are you very far?

No longer standing up,
we are now down on our knees.
Have mercy on us, forgive us,
it's You we want to please.

We've sinned against You,
but we want a fresh, new start.
We say 'Jesus is our Lord,
please come into our heart."

I chose the title for this poem, for two reasons. One, life has changed for everyone since the Corona Virus outbreak. And two, when we choose to invite Jesus into our lives, we are changed forever.

Thrive

The enemy tried to squash us down,
he'll soon be gone; he'll leave this town.

Listen for him, he won't be near.
God will wipe each and every tear.

God speaks through you, and He speaks
through me,
He'll welcome us Home, soon, you will see.

He has lit our way toward the path
of salvation,
and it's His desire that we all be one nation.

Some may listen and some may not.
He'll save those who hear and teach them a lot.

Then this fulfillment will give Him
much pride,
for those who have chosen to be on His side.

"...The earnest prayer of a righteous person has
great power and wonderful results."
~ James 5:16 (NLT)

Will You?

Love is just waiting to be found,
It makes your head turn upside down.

Time and devotion are the best gifts of all.
Their cost is priceless – not found in a mall.

To the outsider, it doesn't make much sense.
It's time to get off of that white picket fence.

Hearts and flowers, some white and
some pink,
A great big smile and even a wink.

Love makes you do some crazy little things,
Making your heart feel like it has wings.

The day has come – let them know
how you feel,
No longer a dream – it's time to get real.

So down you go on one of your knees,
"Together, forever, say yes... will you please?"

*"Beloved, let us love one another, for love is of God; and
everyone who loves is born of God and
knows God." ~ 1 John 4:7*

Straight Ahead

Time is of the essence; it's quickly going by.
He'll be here real soon, so there's
no need to cry.

Going back Home to my place up above,
I'll see those I've missed, those I really did love.

"Grampa, Gramma, I knew you'd be here!"
The path wasn't easy, but He made it so clear.

He knew I'd be here, on this very fine day.
Because I trusted and followed The Way.

There's no turning back now, I'll forge
straight ahead,
"Jesus, it's true, it's all like You said!"

Give thanks to the Lord, for He is good,
I really do love this new 'neighborhood.'

*"Eye has not seen, nor ear heard, nor have entered into
the heart of man the things which God has prepared for
those who love Him." ~ 1 Corinthians 2:9*

Quotes to Uplift & Inspire

"Whether you think you can or think you can't, you're right." — **Henry Ford**

"God would not have put a dream in your heart, if He hadn't already given you everything you need to fulfill it."
— **Joel Osteen**

"It's not the size of the dog in the fight. It's the size of the fight in the dog." — **unknown**
(Just like David when he fought Goliath)

"You cannot give up – God is not finished."
—**unknown**

"Don't get discouraged, it may be the last key on the ring that opens the door." — **unknown**

"When you look down all you see is dirt, so keep looking up." — **unknown**

"Being a Christian is neither an event nor a quick fix. Rather it is a journey. There are things for us to learn along the way."
— **Charles Stanley**

"Small changes make a big impact."
— u**nknown**

"There are no dreams too large, no innovation unimaginable and no frontiers beyond our reach." — **John S. Herrington**

"One of the greatest discoveries a man makes, one of his great surprises, is to find he can do what he was afraid he couldn't do."
—**Henry Ford**

"If you risk failure, then you also risk success."
— **Tom Hiddleston**

"The best way to predict the future is to create it**.**" — **Abraham Lincoln**

"Don't be surprised if you end up somewhere you never intended to go. In the end, you will discover it is right where you belong."
— **unknown**

"The earth has music for those who listen."
—**William Shakespeare**

"Often when you think you're at the end of something, you're at the beginning of something else." — **Mr. Rogers**

"As one person I cannot change the world, but I can change the world of one person."
— **Paul Shane Spear**

"Down, but not out." – **Charles Stanley**

"You and you alone are the only person who can live the life that writes the story that you were meant to tell." — **Kerry Washington**

"Sorrow looks back, worry looks around, faith looks up." — **unknown**

"Faith is thanking God before it happens."
— **Mark Batterson**

"Keep on, keeping on!" — **unknown**

"Everyone has a much larger job, than just their trade." – **From "The Chosen" series**

"Faith your fears." — **John Gray**

"Don't fight people, let God do it."
— **Charles Stanley**

"You can't hurry it up, and nothing can stop it!" (re: Jesus' return) – **Jentezen Franklin**

"Life is like being at the movies. When it's over you go home." – **Mark Woulas**

Easy as A.B.C.

"You did not choose Me, but I chose you...."
~ John 15:16

We all have one thing in common – a birthday. Our Creator predestined us to have a certain day to be born, and that date can never be changed. We also have another thing in common — Jesus calls out for us to be born a second time. This time we have the choice over what date that will be. He also has a special plan for each of our lives. It is predestined for us. All we have to do is answer His call and receive His Holy Spirit.

We all have a specific purpose in this life. God created us that way, and He wants us to go on the journey of discovering what that calling is.

*"For by Him all things were created that are in heaven and that are on earth, visible and invisible... **All** things were created **through** Him and **for** Him."* — *Colossians 1:16 [emphasis added]*

Not only were we created **through** God, but we were also created **for** God. We are not here to sit around all day playing video games. We have kingdom work to do here, in preparation for the day we go Home to Jesus. We each have a specific mission for Christ. It is up to us to discover what exactly that is. Because of Colossians 1:16, I had been asking God continually, "What am I here for? What do You want me to do? I need to know what my purpose is! I want to know so that I can start doing it!"

Before leaving to go on a retreat in New Hampshire, I had asked the Lord if He would finally reveal my purpose to me while I was there. At the retreat, I was walking on a path, on my way to the cabin. I found a pen on the ground, picking it up as I went on my merry way. Once I was home though, I was reflecting about the retreat. I remembered picking up that pen, and when I picked it up, a very gentle voice had said, *"I want you to write."* I heard the Holy Spirit once (without realizing it). Then I heard Him a second time, once I was home reflecting on the retreat. It was kind of like... an echo.

We will not know what our calling is until we answer yes to Jesus. He is continually calling out, inviting us to be a part of His family. If we choose not to, we will lose out on living the abundant life that we were predestined for and miss spending eternity with Him in Heaven. We just need to trust Him... there has never been anyone more in love with us, than Jesus is. We just need to say 'yes' to His invitation.

It's as easy as A.B.C. ADMIT we have sinned (we all do). *1 John 1:8-9 (NLT)* says, *"If we say we have no sin, we are only fooling ourselves and refusing to accept the truth. But if we confess our sins to Him, He is faithful and just to forgive us and to cleanse us from every wrong."*

Next, we need to BELIEVE that Jesus died on the cross to pay the penalty for our sins, not His sins, because He was perfect. He was the spotless lamb, sacrificially given up for us. *"For God decided to save us through our Lord Jesus Christ, not to pour out His anger on us. He died for us so that we can live with Him forever..."* ~ *1 Thessalonians 5:9-10*

Next, we need to be willing to COMMIT our life to Him, and to serve Him here, until He takes us Home to Heaven. *"But you are a **chosen** generation, a royal priesthood, a holy nation, His own special people, that you may proclaim the praises of Him who **called** you out of darkness into His marvelous light..."* ~ *1 Peter 2:8-10 [emphasis added]*

If you would like to make Jesus the Lord of your life, you can say this prayer, or use your own words:

Dear Jesus, I come before You today to tell You that I am truly sorry for all the times I have sinned against You. Thank You so much for dying on the cross for me – paying the penalty for all my sins. I want to be able to hear You now, so I'm asking You to send me Your Holy Spirit so that I may serve You. Thank You, Jesus. Amen

When you accept Jesus into your life you can begin going on a journey of discovering what

God's will is for your life. It's an exciting process! I recommend that your next step is to tell someone who can help you find a Bible-based church and also get your hands on a Bible and dig in. Then be amazed as you hear from God in a new and exciting way. Remember, there's JOY in the JOurneY.

After reading this book I am sure you will now find reasons why you can sing too. I suggest you go back to the beginning and read "The Voice of the Shepherd" poem again, for inspiration. Your story is totally different than anyone else's.

"We don't decide, we discover God's plan for us." – Jentezen Franklin says.

So now, *"**Arise!** Then live YOUR story!"*

Made in the USA
Middletown, DE
09 October 2021

49489397R00047